Dear Parent:
Your child's love of reading starts here!

Every child learns to read in a different way and at his or her own speed. You can help your young reader improve and become more confident by encouraging his or her own interests and abilities. You can also guide your child's spiritual development by reading stories with biblical values and Bible stories, like I Can Read! books published by Zonderkidz. From books your child reads with you to the first books he or she reads alone, there are I Can Read! books for every stage of reading:

SHARED READING
Basic language, word repetition, and whimsical illustrations, ideal for sharing with your emergent reader.

BEGINNING READING
Short sentences, familiar words, and simple concepts for children eager to read on their own.

READING WITH HELP
Engaging stories, longer sentences, and language play for developing readers.

READING ALONE
Complex plots, challenging vocabulary, and high-interest topics for the independent reader.

ADVANCED READING
Short paragraphs, chapters, and exciting themes for the perfect bridge to chapter books.

I Can Read! books have introduced children to the joy of reading since 1957. Featuring award-winning authors and illustrators and a fabulous cast of beloved characters, I Can Read! books set the standard for beginning readers.

A lifetime of disc~~over~~~~begity institute libraryords~~ "I Can Read!"
~~Peabody, MA 01960~~

Visit www.icanread.com for information on enriching your child's reading experience.
Visit www.zonderkidz.com for more Zonderkidz I Can Read! titles.

Today salvation has come to your house.
Luke 19:9 NIrV

ZONDERKIDZ

Zaccheus Meets Jesus
Copyright © 2011 by Crystal Bowman
Illustrations © 2011 by Valerie Sokolova

Requests for information should be addressed to:
Zonderkidz, *Grand Rapids, Michigan 49530*

Library of Congress Cataloging-in-Publication Data

Bowman, Crystal.
      Zaccheus / written by Crystal Bowman ; illustrated by Valerie Sokolova.
        p. cm.
      ISBN 978-0-310-72673-9 (softcover)
      1. Zaccheus (Biblical figure)—Juvenile literature.   I. Sokolova, Valerie, ill. II. Title.
BS2520.Z3B69 2012
226.4'09505—dc23   2011030590

Editor: *Mary Hassinger*
Art Direction: *Jody Langley*

Printed in China
16 17 18 /DSC/ 10 9 8 7 6 5

ZONDERkidz I Can Read! 1 BEGINNING READING

Zacchaeus Meets Jesus

story by Crystal Bowman
pictures by Valerie Sokolova

4

Once there was a rich man
named Zacchaeus (Za-KEE-us).
He lived in the city of Jericho.

The people had to pay their taxes
to Zacchaeus.

Sometimes Zacchaeus took too much
money from them.
So the people did not like him.

One day Jesus came to Jericho.

He walked into the city.

A big crowd of people
followed Jesus.

Some of the people were sick.

They wanted Jesus to

make them better.

Some were blind.

They wanted Jesus to touch their eyes

so they could see again.

Some wanted to hear his stories.

And some just wanted to see Jesus.

12

Zacchaeus wanted to see Jesus too.

But there were too many people
around Jesus.

Zacchaeus was a short man.

He could not see over the people.

"I know what to do!" Zacchaeus said.

"I will climb a tree.

Then I will be able to see Jesus."

So that is what Zacchaeus did.

15

Zacchaeus sat in a tree

by the side of the road.

He saw Jesus

coming toward him.

Jesus walked closer to the tree.

He looked up in the tree

and saw Zacchaeus.

"Zacchaeus!" said Jesus.

"Hurry!

Come down from the tree.

I am going to your house."

19

Zacchaeus was surprised!

"How does Jesus know my name?"

he said.

He was happy that Jesus wanted

to come to his house.

Zacchaeus climbed down the tree
as fast as he could.

Then he walked with Jesus

to his house.

But the people were not happy.

"Why does Jesus want to go

to his house?" they asked.

"Zacchaeus is a bad man!"

Zacchaeus and Jesus

went inside the house.

26

Then Zacchaeus told Jesus,

"I will give half of my money

to poor people.

And I will give back four times

what I took from people."

Jesus was glad that he went
to visit Zacchaeus.
Jesus knew that Zacchaeus
was sorry for his sins.

29

30

Jesus said to Zacchaeus,

"You are saved today.

Now you are part of my family.

I have come to save

people like you."

Zacchaeus was so happy

that Jesus had come to his house.

After that day, Zacchaeus wanted

to do what was right.